How To Protect Your Faith

How To Protect Your Faith

by
Norvel Hayes

HARRISON HOUSE
Tulsa, Oklahoma

Unless otherwise indicated,
all Scripture quotations are taken from
the *King James Version* of the Bible.

3rd Printing
Over 20,000 in Print

How To Protect Your Faith
ISBN 0-89274-279-8
Copyright © 1983 by Norvel Hayes
P. O. Box 1379
Cleveland, Tennessee 37311
(formerly ISBN 0-917726-19-7)

Published by Harrison House, Inc.
P. O. Box 35035
Tulsa, Oklahoma 74153

Printed in the United States of America.
All rights reserved under International Copyright Law.
Contents and/or cover may not be reproduced in whole or in part in any form without the express written consent of the Publisher.

TABLE OF CONTENTS

Chapter

1	WHAT IS FAITH?	5
2	HOW TO PROTECT YOUR FAITH WITH JOY	15
3	HOW TO PROTECT YOUR FAITH WITH GIVING	27
4	SPEAK TO THE MOUNTAIN	39
5	BE YE A DOER OF THE WORK	45
6	PROTECT YOUR FAITH WITH LOVE	55
7	PROTECT YOUR FAITH WITH WORSHIP	63
	EPILOGUE	72

CHAPTER ONE

WHAT IS FAITH?

Faith brings God's power for whatever you need
. . . into your life
. . . into your body
. . . into your business
. . . into your mind
. . . into your spirit
. . . into your children

Your faith will bring his blessing to you for whatever you are believing God to do for you.

Now God won't ever leave you nor forsake you, but he says in his word that the only way you can please him is with faith.

> *For without faith, it is impossible to please God (Hebrews 11:6).*

Impossible . . . that means it can't be done! You can't please God with your life and begin to have his abundant life flowing through you if you don't have faith. The Bible says in Hebrews 11:1 that *"Faith is the substance of things hoped for, the evidence of things not seen."* Romans 10:17 says, *"So then faith cometh by hearing, and hearing by the word of God."* You can't get faith any other way. If you would ask me to pray for you to have faith, I would say, "No, I can't do that." Faith comes by hearing God's word and receiving his word as truth in your heart. You must hear God's word! Then faith will come.

I watched a Vicki Jamison television program recently. She had guests who were putting on a passion play about Jesus dying on the cross. An unbeliever went in to see the play and gave his life to the Lord. He had never believed in Jesus before he saw the play. But he got a little vision of the price that Jesus paid for his sins, and it touched his heart. If that can't touch your heart, I don't know what in the world can... somebody dying for you, taking all the beating and suffering for you for hours, just so you can get saved. But God gives you the faith to believe to be saved. From then on, you get faith by hearing his word, receiving it into your heart and doing what it says.

In most churches today, it's difficult to get people to come out to hear the word of God. In the scriptures, it says multitudes came out to hear Jesus. Multitudes and multitudes came. Today, they just don't come. Someone spoke to me about a meeting T. L. Osborn had over in Africa. They said blind eyes were opened, devils came out of people and cripples walked by the dozens.

"Uh huh," I said. "How many were there?"

"70,000."

"Oh, seventy thousand you say. Where was the meeting held?"

"Out in a field in the burning hot sun. They had to stand up. They came from miles and miles."

Well, if you had a meeting in a field here in America out in the burning hot sun, miles from town, and the

What Is Faith?

folks had to walk to the meeting and stand up the whole time, how many people do you think would come? They just wouldn't come, that's all.

So, no cripples will walk.

No blind eyes will be opened.

No devils will come out of people. You can hardly get people to come to a nice comfortable church to hear the word. We are so gospel-hardened here in America, to get 70,000, you've got to have a mailing list, advertise on radio and television, pass out handbills door-to-door, have a crusade committee meeting once or twice a week for a year, and then, if the weather isn't bad, you will maybe get two thousand out the first night. If you are just going to have a one-night meeting, you've got to have a popular speaker, a good singing group and serve a good dinner. Then the folks will say, "Oh, look who is going to sing! Look who is going to speak! I think I will go."

Who are they going to see? Jesus?

Forget it! So, Jesus won't be able to do very much. Those 70,000 people in Africa came to hear about Jesus and to trust him by faith. And when they heard, they believed and got their miracles. At meetings in America, God will send forth a little bit of his healing power even though I wonder how he can when the unbelief is so high. Jesus *"did not many mighty works there because of their unbelief" (Matthew 13:58).*

But, God loves us, and you can get a little something from these meetings. Cripples won't walk off, though, as a rule. Oh, I see cripples walk from time to time. God still has the power, you know. Not too long ago, Archie Dennis and I were holding a service in a Lutheran church in New York. The very first night, a cripple walked. He just dropped his crutches and walked off. We passed by a blind boy, and his eyes popped open. The pastor was going to leave on vacation the next day while I was holding the meetings for him, but he said to me, "I think I'll stay. This is really getting interesting!"

God still has the power, but he only releases the power when he finds faith. Otherwise the power just stays in heaven. That is the way he has it set up. Isaiah 55:8 says, *"For my thoughts are not your thoughts, neither are my ways your ways, saith the Lord."* Since he is God, we should let him do things his way. A lot of people don't have very much respect for God. They won't let him be God, so they don't get very much from him. They just stumble around, professing that they have faith, and then keep wondering why nothing they believe for comes to pass.

Why doesn't it come to pass? Why doesn't it come to pass?

Why don't I get healed?

Why don't my children get saved?

Why doesn't my business prosper?

Well, let God be God! Start doing things his way! He can prosper everything you put your hands on. You have to read the Bible, and let faith begin to operate in your life. Your attitude about God can change your whole life. Your faith in him releases the power. Jesus used to go up into the mountains, out from the city. The people would follow him.

They would climb the mountains to see him.

If you were a sick person, and you knew that Jesus was up on a mountain someplace outside the city, and you knew that if you could get to him, you would be

What Is Faith?

healed, and your faith takes you up the mountain to see him
   . . . just watch out
   . . . you are going to be healed!

If you know a blind person, you take him where Jesus is. Tell him that when he gets to Jesus, he will be able to see. Then, when he gets to Jesus, his eyes will pop open!

You say, where is Jesus?

Well, Jesus should be in his CHURCH.

The Bible says in Ephesians 1:22 and 23 that the CHURCH is his body. But you can't find very many churches that are attached to Jesus in any way today and who believe he heals the crippled and blind. Jesus is supposed to be the head of the church, and YOU are the church.

His body — his hands — his power on the earth.

If you love Jesus, you shouldn't stand for your church to even have its doors open unless it is a place where people can come and get whatever they need — just like they used to go to Jesus and EVERY ONE would be healed and have devils cast out of them. They believed the word of God. Anything except victory is not Jesus. Don't try and change him.

Jesus is still the word of God today. The Bible is God's Law Book.

He *was* the word and he *is* the word and he *will always be* the word. St. John in the very first chapter says:

> *In the beginning was the Word and the Word was with God and the Word was God . . . and the Word was made flesh, and dwelt among us.*

Those who heard the word that Jesus preached and then believed what he said, received whatever they needed.

God says in the sixteenth chapter of Mark to lay hands on sick people, and they will recover. People in most churches don't lay hands on the sick, so they don't recover. They just say, "I'll be praying for you." However, the book of James says to be a *doer* of the word, not just a hearer only. BE YE A *DOER* OF THE WORD.

Lay hands on the sick people.

God does the healing part.

You just have to lay the hands on them.

You are Jesus' hands.

If Jesus were here, that's what he would do.

If you are going to be a doer of the word, you have to pick up your hands and lay them down on sick people. Don't try to make anything else out of it, because you won't get away with it. You will just be deceiving yourself, and people won't get healed.

I ask church people all the time, "Do you know what your hands are? Well, they are those two wide things down there at the end of your arms. You are supposed to pick them up and lay them down."

"Where?" they ask.

"On sick people. Can't you read?"

Some people look at me real funny when I ask them if they can read. They act to me like they don't know how.

Well, the Bible says to lay hands on the sick, and they will get well. Any part of the Bible a person obeys, is the part he gets. Any part of the Bible you refuse to do, is the part you don't get and in that part of your life you will continue to suffer.

What Is Faith?

If you make up your mind that God means what he says in Third John, verse 2, that he wants you to be in health and prosper even as your soul prospers; that God is the head, and you are a part of the Church, and as a part of God, you can be successful and healthy
 ... then, you will be successful in everything you do,
 ... and healthy in every part of your body.

Thinking that God wants you poor in order for you to be humble is a lie of the devil. You can be just as humble rich as you can be poor. Humbleness doesn't have anything to do with money. It is an attitude of your spirit, not your natural circumstances. Every person that is a doer of the word and not just a hearer only, will receive the blessings of God
 ... financially and
 ... every other way.

You have to have faith in order to have your faith protected. And to get the faith, you must hear and *believe* God's word. Stop listening to the words of men and start hearing the word of God.

That's where to start.

Get out your Bible and start reading it with the idea of believing every single word, exactly the way it says, and start doing what it says.

You probably already are a person of faith.

You have renewed your mind in the word of God and have your faith built real strong in your inner man.

You can quote scriptures and you are "living by faith." Now,

God is going to put your faith to a test.

That's right.

He will put it to a test.

That's how he — and you — find out how strong your faith is.

If you want God's bountiful blessings to fall on you and to flow in you all the time, your faith will have to pass God's test. Not my test or your test; God's test. God will promote you, if he can trust you. If he can't trust you, he will never promote you. God will even give you money if he can trust you with it. He will make you rich. He will give you spiritual gifts. He will open up the treasures of the spirit world to you. People ask all the time: Why doesn't God bless his people more? Because he cannot trust them. They can't pass his test.

His test is his word.

The last time the Lord gave me $200,000 dollars, I said, "Lord, what am I going to do with it? I don't need it. What did you give it to me for?"

He said, "You passed my test!"

I said, "Passed your test? Passed your test? What in the world did I do to pass your test?"

He said, "You fulfilled a scripture. Tell the churches everywhere you go ... tell them ... that the Bible is my test; every time they fulfill a scripture, tell them to never worry about the answers to their prayers.

The answers will automatically be there. James 2:23 says:

> And the scripture was fulfilled which saith, Abraham believed God, and it was imputed unto him for righteousness: and he was called the Friend of God.

Abraham fulfilled the scriptures by believing that what God had said would come to pass. Abraham waited twenty-five years for God to do what he said he would.

What Is Faith?

How long have you waited and not doubted God? James 1:8 says *"a double minded man is unstable in all his ways,"* and doesn't get anything from God. But if we stand steadfast in faith, until we pass God's test, not doubting, then the blessings of God begin to flow to us.

And they flow . . .
And they flow . . .
And they flow.

People across the country say to me, "Brother Norvel, why does God bless you with these things all the time, and it is so easy for you to get the blessings? How can you operate several businesses and still teach twenty nights a month?"

"Well," I say, "I don't use the blessings against God. If he gives me $20,000 this week on a deal, I don't stop passing out tracts at the airport. I just go to my next speaking engagement and cast devils out of people. I will still take time with the one who has the lonely heart. If I come across someone who is hungry, I will feed him. That one that no one else will help, I will take time with."

And now I am getting to the part I want to teach you about, because

. . . your faith may be a dead faith,
. . . your faith may not have any love,
. . . your faith may have respect of persons,
. . . your faith may not be a doer of the work,
. . . your faith may not be protected.

You may claim things, and it will seem like it takes so long for it to happen.

In these next few chapters, I will show you some things that will make your faith work real easy. You can know the blessings of God in your life in a measure you never thought possible. You will pass God's tests and be a bright light to the church and to the world. You will learn to live in the glory of God. Philippians 4:19 says, *"But my God shall supply all your need according to his riches in glory by Christ Jesus."*

You are listening to a man who has learned to live in the GLORY of God. I mean in the GLORY! Read and listen with your heart, and let God show you how to enter into the realm in him that he desires for all of his children. Jesus said in John 10:10, *"I am come that they might have life, and that they might have it more abundantly,"* NOW — in this time. Let us begin.

CHAPTER TWO

HOW TO PROTECT YOUR FAITH WITH JOY

The Book of James, in the first and second chapters, is absolutely wonderful to teach you how to protect your faith. James gives many things to do and many things not to do. Study it over and over again, until it sinks way down deep inside of you. It begins:

> *James, a servant of God and of the Lord Jesus Christ, to the twelve tribes which are scattered abroad, greeting.*
>
> *My brethren, count it all joy when ye fall into divers temptations...*

Okay, let's stop right there.

Do you count it all joy when temptation comes to you?

God begins to test your faith. You have a temptation to doubt God.

You begin to wonder if it is going to come to pass.

Do you count it all joy? Or do you get all sad and depressed and get to wondering and wondering?

That's not God. That's the devil and you.

God says, count it all joy! Rejoice!

Is the devil trying to undercut your faith? Make you doubt? Yes. You know, the devil doesn't want you to have a relationship with God. That's the reason he comes to tempt you to doubt God's word. He did it to Eve. He tempted her by saying, "you won't die if you eat the fruit." Well, God had said she would. Then the devil said she wouldn't. Who to believe? It is a temptation. James says to count it all joy to be tested to believe God's word. Oh, praise God forevermore!

Some of you might have heard Brother Kenneth Hagin tell about when his children would get sick, he would say to the Lord, "Thank you, Jesus, for another chance to believe your word." You see, before he would ever pray, he would "count it all joy," and sometimes they would be healed before he would even be through saying it. God can heal quickly. Just throw your hands up in the air and begin to praise God. It is a terrible thing to see your child sick. But if you will stand strong right in the midst of the temptation to doubt, and count it all joy . . .

"Brother Norvel! Count it all joy that my child is sick?"

No! Count it all joy that you have another opportunity to believe God's word!

God says in Psalm 103:3, *"Who forgiveth all thine iniquities; who healeth all thy diseases."* When he says ALL, he means ALL. Not just some of them, sometimes. All means ALL. Begin to praise God. Oh Jesus, thank you for this chance to trust you. Thank you for this opportunity to see your power released to earth from heaven for my child. Thank you for healing my baby and making him well. Usually, it won't be five minutes before the child is healed. And if it takes longer — Abraham waited 25 years — continue to count it all joy.

God's word is true.

Numbers 23:19 says:

> *God is not a man, that he should lie; neither the son of man, that he should repent: hath he said, and shall he not do it? or hath he spoken, and shall he not make it good?*

God himself says in Isaiah 46:11:

> *I have spoken it, I will also bring it to pass; I have purposed it, I will also do it.*

If temptation comes upon you, count it all joy! I don't mean sadness. Sadness is the opposite of joy. The Bible says JOY. Act like you are joyful, you are happy. It is a JOY to believe God's word. But if you begin to be sad and start thinking and saying with your mouth, "Oh God, Oh God, what am I going to do? This is so terrible!" and you walk around with a sad face and tell everyone your troubles and your unhappy circumstances, then you will wait a long time getting any answer to your prayer for help.

The joy of the Lord is your strength (Neh. 8:10) in a trial of your faith. When God puts your faith to its test, the joy of the Lord will carry you through. Joy protects your faith. Wrap your faith up in joy and your faith will stay strong and bring the power of God to you.

Ken Copeland was trying to get his plane at a time when his wife had been listening to quite a few of my tapes. Ken said to me,

> "I was trying to get that plane, and the money wasn't coming in. I think I had

prayed in about $60,000 and the plane was to be delivered soon. I had to have the rest of the money. I was playing one of your tapes, and you started yelling over the tape. You said God had told you that your faith was not pleasing him, and that you had to repent. You said you had been wondering when he was going to do a certain thing. You said that with your mind, you were wondering when he was going to do it. You said that God said you were out of his will, and that you were actually hindering him from bringing it to pass with your doubt. He finally said it would not come to pass.

Ken continued,

"The Holy Ghost jumped up in me and started yelling at me, 'You listen to him, you listen to him; that's just what you are doing. That's why you have this plane bogged down. You have been wondering why God doesn't send the money and where he was going to bring it from.

"I hadn't realized that I was wondering like that until the Lord showed me with that tape of yours. I did just what you had to do. I had to repent. I repented and began to rest in the Lord."

Ken told me that as he began to count it all joy to have his faith tested, it wasn't long before the plane was completely his.

One time the Lord said to me, "Son, you go around the country for me, teaching the people faith. You teach for me and show the people how to have faith, but I wish you would learn how yourself."

Can you imagine?

God said he wished I would learn about faith myself!

Here I was seeing people healed and saved and was receiving great financial miracles in my own life, and he said he wished I would really learn what faith was. At that time, I was wondering about this certain thing I wanted God to do for me. And I wasn't stilling my mind and protecting my faith with joy. I was wondering why God didn't hurry up and do it. God told me it wasn't any of my business how or when he did anything. He said that when I began to wonder about the when's and the how's of it, I doubted. Doubt cut off his power from working on my behalf. Count it all joy and protect your faith by praising God and trusting him completely for the answer. Then watch out! Blessings will sneak up from behind and knock you down. Then you can wonder how easy it was for God to do it. Your faith will have passed God's test of joy.

People have the hardest time believing God for financial blessings. I know pastors who have great financial problems in their churches. They look at their 27 member congregation and say, "What am I going to do?" Young pastors just starting out, just out of Bible school, full of faith, full of zeal, begin a work for God, and wham — here comes the trial of their faith. Or let's say, you give your business to God and say you are going to believe God for financial blessings. God prepares a test for you.

The 27 member congregation gives about 25 cents each.

No customers come into your business.
What are you going to do?
Can you stand right in the middle of that mess and count it all joy?
What if it is a great test, and a day comes when you and your wife sit down to beans for dinner? Do you praise God for the beans and this opportunity to trust him?
"Oh, Brother Norvel," you say, "I don't know if I could praise God for beans or not."
Well, you will have to pass God's test.
You say, "Well, I believe God has better things than that for me."
That's right. And your faith will get them for you, too.
But, God will put your faith to a test. And if you will count it all joy and let your faith wear the garment of praise, the financial blessings will come.
It has to come.
You have fulfilled a scripture. James 1:2 is yours.
When you fulfill scripture, God does his part.
He brings the blessing to you.
You must make your mind be still and know that God is God. You begin to wonder when will this blessing fall?
... when will it fall?
... when will it fall?
It will fall whenever you pass God's test.
You say, "Oh, I want it now. I want it now."
BE QUIET. Just stand steadfast and show God your faith and count it all joy. I guarantee you, it will fall.
IT WILL FALL.
It falls all the time on me.

How To Protect Your Faith With Joy

Where's it coming from? Where's it coming from?

BE QUIET. Make your mind be still. You'll never know where it is coming from, if God has anything to do with it. It will just appear. GLORY BE TO GOD FOREVERMORE. It will just appear.

Let's continue with James 1:3:

> *Knowing this, that the trying of your faith worketh patience.*

Now we see what God is trying to do with us in this test. He wants to develop patience in us. I tell you this for a fact. The patience of God will drive the devil crazy.

Did you get that?

The patience of God will drive the devil crazy.

That's right. It drives him crazy. If you are going to cast a devil out of somebody, and it acts like it isn't going to come out ... "I won't come out, I won't come out!" ... I just stand there with the patience of God on me and say, "Shut up, you dumb devil. You have to come out, you don't have any choice."

Anytime you get in a hurry, you won't get very much from God. Learn the patience of God. Some people are always in a hurry. It could be their nature to some extent, but they can learn to slow down. You should always know exactly what you are doing and exactly where you are going. If someone tries to hurry you up, and you are not sure about something, stop everything. Don't make a move until you are sure. I don't ever get in a hurry. Brother Kenneth Hagin says I have two speeds: slow, and s-l-o-w-e-r.

I have learned the patience of God. I have let faith have its perfect work in me, just like James says. You can, too. You can let the trying of your faith work

patience in you, if you will count it all joy to be tested, and then James says ... you will be perfect.
... you will be entire,
... lacking nothing.

You see, if you still want things, if there are still needs in your life, then faith has not had its perfect work in you yet. Begin to count it all joy, and let the patience of God come to you. This is how you become perfect. God has told us in his word to be perfect. He would not have told us to be perfect if we could not attain to it. James is showing us how.

A lot of people get scared to death when they go out knocking on doors for Jesus. Knock, knock, knock. "Oh, I hope nobody is home." About thirty seconds go by. "Whew, nobody is home. Guess I can leave." They start for the sidewalk, and the door opens. "Oh, no. They are home." The persons call to you, "Did you want something?"

You see, you are supposed to be standing there with the patience of God on you so you can witness to them about Jesus. You are to be full of joy, trusting Jesus to reach that person through you. If you will let your faith be tried, you will be perfect, wanting nothing. The people will hear the word of God and be transferred from the kingdom of the devil into the kingdom of God. Faith will have produced a perfect work.

Oh, joy and patience will protect your faith. And a protected faith will produce a perfect work for God.

Now, let's say the temptation is toward committing a sin. Of course, doubting God's word is sin, and you will need to repent. But, let's look at some situations that tempt you to commit sins of the flesh. When you see something that is not right for you, stay away from it.

James says in verse thirteen in the first chapter to, first of all, realize that the temptation has not come from God:

> Let no man say when he is tempted, I am tempted of God; for God cannot be tempted with evil, neither tempteth he any man:

You see, Jesus loves you. He will not tempt you. The devil comes to tempt you and to draw you away from God through a lust in your life. James continues:

> But every man is tempted, when he is drawn away of his own lust, and enticed. Then when lust hath conceived, it bringeth forth sin: and sin, when it is finished, bringeth forth death.

Sometimes a person can like their sin so much that they wait too long to come back to the Lord, and then they can't come back.

That's right!

I said, they can't come back.

They just die and go to hell.

You have to watch it about getting into sin. Lots of people want to go to heaven, but they don't want to give up their sin. When you work on the streets, you meet all kinds of them. I guess I'll never forget the girl I met once out on the streets who couldn't come back. I saw her on a corner, and I started to walk up to her. She began to scream at me... "Stay away from me. Go away from me. Don't talk to me. I don't want to talk to you."

"What in the world has happened to you, young lady?"

"Yeah, what's happened to me? What's happened to me? I'll tell you what's happened to me. Would you believe I know what it means to be a goody-goody? I used to sing in the choir. I know what it means to feel God's presence."

"Well, I have no reason not to believe you."

"But I got tired being a good girl. I got tired going to church. I can't never feel God no more. I can't never come back. I am doomed forever."

"No, you're not, honey. Jesus will forgive you. If you want to come back, Jesus will forgive you of your sins. Jesus loves you."

"No! I can't never come back! I got tired being a goody-goody. But, you can do me a favor, will you?"

"What's that?"

"You can tell young people all over the country as you work with them to never get tired working for Jesus. Don't never get tired giving themselves to him. Mister, I live on the streets. You see that girl up there on the next corner, in the white knee boots, pacing back and forth like a mad dog?"

"Yes."

"I am married to that girl. I just got tired being good. I am married to that girl. I just wanted to try a little bit of the world, but I took too big a bite. Now I can't never come back. Just tell the young people, not to get tired working for Jesus."

... and she walked off into the night,

... into the world of the doomed and the damned!

Many people say to me, "Brother Norvel, I have failed God. I have sinned. What should I do?" I say, "You are supposed to repent ... repent ... repent ... REPENT. QUICKLY! REPENT — Jesus will forgive you — <u>NOW</u>!

I hope none of you ever fall. But there may be some who will sin or who have already sinned before God. That sin lays heavy on you. Your faith cannot operate. When the temptation came, your faith was not protected by joy and patience. You gave into the lust and committed sin. Immediately, your spirit was grieved. Your garment of praise became a cloak of heaviness.

QUICKLY, fall on your face. Repent. Cry out to God for forgiveness. Tell him you are sorry. The quicker you repent, the easier it will be to have your joy restored to protect your faith. The longer you wait, the bigger opening you make for the devil to come in and take you over in that area of weakness.

REPENT! NOW — Please don't wait!

God will forgive you immediately and begin to restore you back to your position of faith and righteousness and joy before himself. He can't instantly restore you back to the level of faith you had before you sinned. Remember that.

People will tell me, "Well, I have repented, but I don't have my joy back." I say to them, "You'll have to allow your faith to be re-established before God. It takes time for the condemnation of the sin to be fully cleansed out of your mind and out of your body. You may even have a trial of your faith to know that you have truly been forgiven before God. God forgives us instantly when we ask, but we must forgive ourselves and allow Jesus through the word of God in I John 1:9 to cleanse us from the sin. You must reach that point in your thought-life that the sin which has been forgiven no longer robs you of faith. And when your faith has been fully re-established before the Father, your joy will be full. As you allow the scriptures on forgiveness in the word of God to saturate your mind and your being, your joy will begin to return to you. When there is no longer any condemnation regarding the sin, your joy will be fully restored.

God will restore you back to where you were before. But you have to be patient. You committed sin before God. God hates sin. God is holy. He can't stand sin. When you committed the sin, the sin put out the light of faith. You can commit sin, but you won't pray for the sick anymore. You won't cast out devils. You don't have the faith. God's power is gone. Sin makes the very foundation of your faith fall apart. It crumbles like a house that has been blown up by a bomb. Sin is that bomb. But when you repent, God's holy power will restore you back again to fulness of joy.

David says in Psalm 51:12, *"Restore unto me the joy of my salvation."* In Psalm 16:11, David says that in the presence of the Lord there is fulness of joy.

The joy of the Lord is your strength, the strength of your faith.

Protect your faith with joy.

CHAPTER THREE

HOW TO PROTECT YOUR
FAITH WITH GIVING

It is so sad to see beautiful people who have money, living on that money and not knowing that in a few days they are going to be dead. What good did the money do them? People have absolutely the wrong idea about money. You can't eat more than two T-bones a day. You can ride in only one car at a time. A lot of people want to be "filthy" rich.

Well, if you have it and you listen to God, you are going to give it away.

And if you have it and don't listen to God, you are going to go to hell.

All you are anyway is the boss over it.

It really isn't yours.

You just look over it, you know. The Lord told me one day when I asked him why he was blessing me so much, "If you don't spend it for me, I'll take every bit of it away from you."

He will, too! He knows exactly how to do it.

I had six or seven businesses flourishing and rolling in tremendous financial profits some years ago. I had built quite a kingdom in my own natural strength. You wouldn't think a man like me had a care in the world! I had a different colored Cadillac to drive each day. I had fancy meals every night with candlelight and crystal and beautiful dishes. That's the way I liked it. I wanted it every night. I spent the winter months in beautiful Miami Beach at the yacht club, and I was pretty proud of myself. I never dreamed that my wealth could be taken away by anyone.

Then one day a man by the name of Kenneth Hagin came to town. I was sitting in his service, and he started prophesying. He called my name. God hit me! I broke and began to weep and cry. In that prophecy, God told me that the devil was going to attack my finances. Well, he had attacked everything else I had. I couldn't believe it was true. I thought to myself, "The devil attack my businesses? Are you kidding? I know how to run businesses. Let him attack. Bring him on." He came on, all right. When he did attack them, I wished he hadn't, I can tell you.

My secretary, who had been a good secretary to me for eighteen years, began to steal from me. She stole so much, we had to sell the business. Two or three of my restaurants went broke. People just stopped coming in. I had just developed 300 lots in Florida, and I couldn't even give them away. I had them all paid for and couldn't sell a one. I thought to myself, "Dear me, what kind of a deal is this?" It was the craziest thing I had ever seen. Everything just stopped — all of a sudden.

Well, the prophecy had also told me what to do during this attack. You know, true prophecy is as good as the written word of God. You can stand on it. The Lord told me in the prophecy that if I would pray and

How To Protect Your Faith With Giving

stand steadfast in him and praise him in all things, that I would come through the attack, and I would be financially more successful than I had ever been. I would never know want again.

So, for about three or four years, I just went everywhere, all over the country, telling people about Jesus. I did anything Jesus wanted me to do. I would be introduced as a very successful businessman who loved Jesus and taught people faith and all the time, my own faith was being tested. My businesses wouldn't make a profit!

You know, when you have a bunch of businesses, and none of them is making a profit, you wish you didn't have ANY! Everybody thought I was rich. They didn't know that every one of those businesses, except one, was a curse to me. They had always made a profit for me before, and now they were like that eleventh verse in the first chapter of the book of James:

> ... *the sun is no sooner risen with a burning heat, but it withereth the grass, and the flower thereof falleth, and the grace of the fashion of it perisheth: so shall the rich man fade away in his ways.*

I saw how very perishable the riches of this world are if they have not been established by God through his word. God wishes for us to prosper. But he desires to be the strength of our riches and not have us depend on our own ability and natural talents to make the money. James 2:5 says:

> *Hath not God chosen the poor of this world rich in faith, and heirs of the kingdom which he hath promised to them that love him.*

God made me poor – to make me rich in faith. Then, he showed me how to use my faith to secure his riches.

I want to tell you something about money. I want to first teach you a little about how God wants you to think about money. Most people think that if they had a lot of money, they would really have a good life. But that's not where life is found. The real life of God is found when you become a giver for Jesus, when you begin to pour out your life for others. You become a person whose pride and self is all gone. You bow down before God and worship him as your Lord, willing to do whatever he wants you to do. You will help anyone, anywhere, no matter how long it takes, no matter how insignificant it seems, no matter how much you would perhaps rather be someplace else, doing something else. You become an empty vessel through whom God can pour out his love to a desperate and needy human race. That's the only way you will find life. It is the life of the Lord Jesus Christ, and his life becomes your life. His plans and his desires are the only plans and desires you have. You can say with Paul in Galatians 2:20:

> *I am crucified with Christ: nevertheless I live; yet not I, but Christ liveth in me: and the life which I now live in the flesh I live by the faith of the Son of God, who loved me, and gave himself for me.*

Luke 9:24 says:
> *... for whosoever will lose his life for my sake, the same shall save it.*

Lose your life in Jesus, and you will find the most beautiful life you ever have dreamed of.

Don't look for life anyplace else.

You won't find it.

It's not there.
I have already looked every place.
I looked for it at the golf course.
I looked for it in Cadillac cars sitting in my driveway.
I looked for it in a wealthy home.
I looked for it at the yacht club in Miami Beach.
I looked for it at Broadway stage plays, front row center; theaters and night clubs.
I looked for it in my family. I was a twenty-eight year-old successful American businessman, with a wife that looked like Elizabeth Taylor's sister, a darling blue-eyed, blond-haired little girl who thought I was the greatest person in the world, thousands of dollars in the bank ... and a messed-up mind.
Yes, that's right. A messed-up mind. Life was all confusion. I could not find real life anywhere. You either have life from God or you don't have it. John 1:4, 5 says:

> *In him – in Jesus – was life; and the life was the light of men. And the light shineth in darkness; and the darkness comprehended it not.*

I was in darkness.
My mind was in darkness.
But Jesus came and brought me light.
That light has become my life.
And I now have life, and more abundantly than ever before, because I have Jesus' life.
He took my old one away!
I know what it means to be in a house all alone and have all of my family turn against me. When all of my businesses were a curse to me, my daughter backslid. I

know a little about what Job went through. I lost everything. But, I protected my faith by walking with Jesus, praising him and thanking him, just like I had good sense. I kept giving out of the life of Jesus that was on the inside of me. Oh, thank you Jesus for your life! Glory be to Jesus! Wonderful Jesus!

I just kept on walking with God and giving him my thankfulness for writing my name in the Lamb's Book of Life. I kept telling others of his redeeming and saving love. After about three to four years, God let me know that I had passed his test. And the glory began to fall on me. Praise be to God. When you begin to learn the principle of giving, you will learn the secret of riches.

When you reach out to other people
. . . to give of yourself,
. . . to give of your substance,
. . . to give of your understanding,
. . . to give some of God's love,
. . . then life will come to you.

Life is like a boomerang — you throw it out and it comes back to you. When you give it out, it will come back to you. The more you give away, the more will come back to you. In Jesus there are two things you just can't give away: your life and your money. Try it. You will find out. The more of yourself you give to people who need you, the more of the life of God will come into you. Life will become more exciting all the time . . .
. . . every day
. . . every day
. . . . every day
. . . . . and the peace of God will saturate your whole being.

If you ever stop giving, life will become hard. You will have to struggle. You will begin to live in a kind of a stupor. You will confess the word of God and will wonder why it doesn't come to pass. God doesn't have any sad days. God doesn't have any valleys. He doesn't fall into them. I have climbed up out of enough valleys in my life. I got sick and tired of them. I stayed in valleys while I tried to be just Mr. Nice Guy. You know, I would tell Jesus, "Jesus, I love you, but I don't want to cast out devils. That scares people, and they back away from me. Don't ask me to do that, Jesus. And, oh yes, Jesus, I don't have any time to pass out tracts. I just can't get too involved, you know. It takes too much time away from what I want to do."

Well, after I lost all my businesses, my family and everything, I had all the time in the world to do what Jesus wanted me to do.

. . . I spent all my time working for Jesus.

. . . I went everywhere.

. . . I passed out tracts at the airports.

. . . I cast out devils everywhere I went, regardless of what the people thought.

. . . I obeyed the word of God.

. . . I gave of myself for Jesus to do anything he wanted to do with me.

When you don't give yourself to God to do what he wants to do, you cut yourself off from his life.

Once you begin to learn to give, there are many avenues of giving. James 2:15, 16 says:

> *If a brother or sister be naked, and destitute of daily food, and one of you say unto them, depart in peace, be ye warmed and filled; notwithstanding ye*

> *give them not those things which are needful to the body; what doth it profit?*

Well, what does it profit? It doesn't profit you and it doesn't profit them. You just walk out of the home. You've got two loaves of bread at home, or maybe you've only got one loaf of bread at home. But you just say to the needy one, "Be warmed and filled, I'll be praying for you," you won't go home and get the loaf of bread and cut it in half and take it back to them. You say you have faith. Big deal!

You say you'll pray for them. No use, it won't do any good.

"Just stay warm, brother." With what?

"Just be filled, my brother." Filled with what?

God wants to bless the brother. He wants to use you. Now look at verse 17: *"Even so faith, if it hath not works, is dead, being alone."*

Do you say you have faith? Protect your faith by giving to your brother who is in need. James says if you ignore your brother, your faith is dead. That means it has no life. You don't know anything about life. Life comes from giving.

Your faith is protected and will work for you when you give and give and give and give and give. Luke 6:38 says:

> *Give, and it shall be given unto you; good measure, pressed down, and shaken together, and running over, shall men give into your bosom. For with the same measure that ye mete withal it shall be measured to you again.*

Now that doesn't mean that you are to use all of your substance to feed people. You are to feed them if they are hungry, and then you are supposed to teach them how to get their own food. God doesn't want you to continue to feed them. If you run across someone who is hungry, don't just pat them on the back and tell them you'll be praying for them. That won't help them. If you take some money out of your pocketbook and give it to them or take some food out of your refrigerator and give it to them, God will bless you for it. Whoever comes across your path that is in need, help them. Proverbs 19:17 says:

> *He that hath pity upon the poor lendeth unto the Lord; and that which he hath given will he pay him again.*

You can't outgive the Lord. He gives it back to you. God told me one time to give a woman in a church some money. She came forward later with her whole family, and they gave their lives to Jesus. The Spirit of the Lord came on me and told me to help her, and it changed the whole family's life!

One Christmas I had a visit late at night from a Church of the Brethren pastor, passing through my town. He called me and asked to visit with me on Christmas Eve. I had taught in his church about two or three times. He was on his way to Florida for Christmas. I said, "Pastor, do you want to be blessed of God more than you have ever been blessed before in your life? Stay with me tonight and Christmas Day. I want you to go with me to the Armory tomorrow."

"All right," he said.

We went to the Armory on Christmas Day, and people from all over the county came to get fruits and nuts and candies. Another pastor friend of mine walked over to a woman and said, "What do you need? Can I help you?" She said, "We don't have any food." I was standing with my pastor and we overheard the conversation. My pastor reached in his pocket and got out $10.00 and said, "Here, Norvel, go and buy that woman some groceries."

I said, "Oh, no, you don't! I'm not getting robbed of this blessing. Put that $10.00 back in your pocket!"

The Brethren pastor and I got into his van, and we took this woman to the grocery store. There was one store open on Christmas Day. We were all sitting in the front seat of the van, and the glory of God fell on us. We all broke and began to weep and cry, and this lady gave her heart to Jesus.

When you let God flow through you to others, they can't take it and stay rigid before God. The love of God is the strongest thing in the world. As we met her natural needs, God moved in a mighty way and met her spiritual needs. She went home that day to a house full of food, and her soul full of Jesus. And you know who got the most blessings of all? Of course, The Brethern pastor and I.

Now don't put the blessing out in front and obey in order to get the blessing. You obey the word of God, and the blessing will come. Deuteronomy 28:1, 2 says,

And it shall come to pass, if thou shalt hearken diligently unto the voice of the Lord thy God, to observe and to do all his commandments which I command thee this day, that the Lord thy God will set thee on high above all nations of the earth: And all these blessings shall

> *come on thee, and overtake thee, if thou shalt hearken unto the voice of the Lord thy God.*

The next twelve verses tell you that in all the areas of your life you will be blessed. And it covers every area of your life: yourself, your family, your finances, your whole life. You will be blessed if you will hearken unto the voice of the Lord your God to observe and do all his commandments. The blessings come from behind and overtake you. They fall upon you in so many different ways. You won't be able to tell how they are coming or who they are coming from. They just happen!

Giving of yourself and your substance protects your faith. Begin to give and see how easy life becomes.

CHAPTER FOUR

SPEAK TO THE MOUNTAIN

Did you know that Mark 11:23 says you can have whatsoever you say? In fact, the rest of the scriptures say you absolutely get what you say. Every day you are confessing what you are going to get tomorrow. If you don't like what you had for life today, change what you are saying and you will find that your tomorrows will be different. Proverbs 10:11 says, *"the mouth of a righteous man is a well of life."* Proverbs 18:21 says, *"death and life are in the power of the tongue."* If we are confessing the word of God, we are speaking life to ourselves and to others. If we constantly confess the circumstances, we are speaking death to ourselves and those around us.

I was reading Mark 11:23 one morning early. I guess I have read it hundreds of times:

> *For verily I say unto you, That whosoever shall say unto this mountain, Be thou removed, and be thou cast into the sea; and shall not doubt in his heart, but shall believe that those things which he*

saith shall come to pass; he shall have whatsoever he saith.

I just kept reading it over and over, and like I said, I guess I've read and preached this verse more than any other verse in the Bible. I began to read it again, and I got through the part where it says *"whosoever shall say unto this mountain,"* and the Lord stopped me and said practically right out loud to me in my ear: "Son, people are not talking to the mountains. They are talking to me."

Now, read Mark 11:23 again. When was the last time you had a conversation with the flu? Did you ever hold a conversation with a cancer? You aren't supposed to talk to Jesus about it. You are supposed to talk to the mountain — whatever the mountain is in your life. Now you don't talk, until words come out of your mouth.

Jesus says to "say."

That is talking with your mouth — out loud!

Not thinking thoughts with your mind, but saying words with your mouth.

Speaking unto the mountain!

Stop talking to Jesus about it.

James tell us to be a doer of the word, not just a hearer. You must DO what the word says to do. And Mark 11:23 says to *"SAY to the mountain, be ye removed and be ye cast into the sea."* You have to say, "CANCER, you can't stay in my body. CANCER, you can't kill me." You have to say with your mouth, "I will never die with cancer."

Whatever the mountain is in your life, you must tell it to go, in the name of Jesus. Do you have a financial mountain? Jesus says to say something to the mountain. Start talking to your money. Tell your checkbook to line up with God's word. Talk to your business.

Speak To The Mountain 41

Command customers to come into your business and spend their money there. Talk to the mountain.

If there is a spirit troubling you or troubling your mate or any other member of your family, talk to the spirit. Tell it to go in the name of Jesus. Tell it it can't operate in your home. Tell it it can't operate on your property because you say it can't. When you talk to the mountain in the name of Jesus and tell it to go, it has to go. You can have what you say in faith, nothing doubting.

But Jesus said to me, "Son, they are not talking to the mountains. They keep talking to me."

They say, "Oh God, help me. Remove this sickness from me.

"Oh, Lord, help me. Oh, Jesus, take this away."

Well, that's not going to get you any help, because you are not doing what Jesus told you to do. Be ye a doer of the word. Whatever the word says, you should obey it. Oh, I know that sometimes it seems strange to do what the word says to do. Hebrews says that God calls "things that be not as though they were." Jesus talked to fig trees, storms, devils, fevers, leprosy, even dead men.

Everything he talked to did what he told it to do.

The fig tree withered and died.

The storm was calmed.

The devils were cast out of people.

The fevers left.

The lepers were cleansed, and

the dead men were raised up to life. Jesus says that we now have the power in his name to do what he did. John 14:14 says, *"If ye shall ask anything in my name, I will do it."* How much more simple could he make it. Speak to the mountain in his name, and tell it what to do. Jesus makes it do what you say.

The next time you feel like you are taking the flu, or feel a cold coming on, talk to that flu or cold, and say, "FLU, I am not going to let you come into my body. Go from me in the name of Jesus. Nose, I tell you in the name of Jesus to stop running. Cough, I tell you to go in the name of Jesus." Are you in pain anyplace? Talk to the pain. Say, "PAIN, I tell you in the name of Jesus to go from me." Is your right arm acting up? Say, "RIGHT ARM, I tell you to stop your rebellion, and act normally, in the name of Jesus."

You can talk to the mountains that are in your children's lives. If the child lives in your home and is under your authority, and a fever takes hold of him, tell the fever to go. I just love to pray for little children. When people come to me and want me to pray for their child who has a fever, I scream at that fever, "YOU FEVER, come out of this child right now, in the name of Jesus." And the fever will break right that minute, and the child will be perfectly fine.

Now, you must speak to the devil with authority. The devil doesn't listen to weak people. You must know that you have the authority in the name of Jesus to tell any mountain of any kind to go, and it must obey you, because Jesus says it will. You see, you are not as strong as the devil yourself. But in the name of Jesus, you are the number one power. You are in Christ, seated at the right hand of God the Father, far above all other powers including the devil and all his cohorts who are under your feet (Ephesians 1:20-22). Once you make up your mind that you are going to have what the Bible says you can have, and that you have the authority to get it through the name of Jesus, and you open up your mouth and begin to say with

your mouth, "It is mine because God says so," and you say with your mouth for the devil to take his hands off whatever you want.
   . . . to take his hands off your marriage,
   . . . off your business,
   . . . off your children,
   . . . to get out of your body,
   . . . then the devil has to do what you say.
   God confirms his word with signs following.

There has been a lot of teaching concerning our confession as God's children and making sure what we say is in line with what the Bible says. That is very good. But a lot of times I hear people going around with a cold or a sickness just confessing 1 Peter 2:24: *"By whose stripes, ye were healed. — By his stripes, I am healed,"* and they have never spoken to the cold or sickness and told it to go. It is very good to confess that you are healed. But you can get healed a lot quicker if you will talk to the mountain first and then confess that you are healed. The more that you have the whole of the counsel of God working on your behalf, the better your life is going to be.

If you have prayed for something and didn't get it, and if Jesus were to walk into the room, and you asked him about it, do you know what he would do? He would quote you chapter and verse. The answers to everything are in the Bible. He would just quote to you the chapter and verse in the Bible that would give you the answer. A friend of mine had a lady tell her that her 20 year old granddaughter was in the last stages of leukemia, a disease that destroys the blood. This Holy-Spirit-filled grandmother prayed to Jesus and asked him for a verse of scripture for her granddaughter. Jesus gave her Ezekiel 16:6:

> *And when I passed by thee, and saw thee polluted in thine own blood, I said unto thee when thou wast in thy blood, Live; yea, I said unto thee when thou wast in thy blood, Live.*

She began to read this scripture to her granddaughter who was in a coma, in the intensive-care section of the hospital. She read and confessed this scripture to her for eight hours that day. The next day, the doctor came in and told them that he couldn't understand it. They had not expected her to last through the night, and yet, the tests were now showing that the blood was much improved. They now expected her to Live. Well, wasn't that what the Lord said? "Live."

Speaking to the mountain, and then confessing God's word will protect your faith, and bring you to live in the glory of God where you have all sufficiency for all things.

CHAPTER FIVE

BE YE A DOER OF THE WORK

In the Summer of 1976, I was teaching at Kenneth Hagin's Bible School. It was the end of the semester. All year, the students had been taught faith by Kenneth Hagin and Ken Copeland as well as other outstanding Bible teachers. It was for these sessions that the Lord gave me these ways to protect your faith which I am sharing with you in this book. The students had their faith built real high, and Jesus wanted them to have these ways to keep their faith protected so they could receive the blessings from him and not have to struggle.

One morning, as I was up early meditating in order to prepare for that day's teaching, I was reading in the first chapter of the book of James. Verse 25 jumped out at me. God underlined the word work in that verse:

> *But whoso looketh into the perfect law of liberty, and continueth therein, he being not a forgetful hearer, but a doer of the* work, *this man shall be blessed in his deed.*

Okay, look at that middle part again... "*he, being not a forgetful hearer, but a doer of the work...*". Then the Lord said to me, "Son, my people get this verse mixed up with verse 22. They quote them the same. They think it says 'but be ye doers of the <u>word</u>' in both verses. But in verse 25, I say to be a 'doer of the <u>work</u>.' "

Did you get that? We must be doers of the word of God, or else our faith is a dead faith. But to be blessed in our deeds, we must also be doers of the work. And you can protect your faith by being a doer of the work and thereby allowing God to bless you in all your deeds. The devil can rob you of your faith if he can get you to stop working for God. You must not stop working for him. How do you work for God? You pray for the sick, you cast out devils, you do whatever the Bible says to do – that's how you work for God. "Well," you say, "I'll work for him, but I am not going to cast out devils."

One Saturday night, I was speaking at a Holiday Inn. There was a devil worshipper in the meeting. She was sitting over on my left, and I knew she was there. I did not know, however, that she had been drinking human blood. She had been beaten by the others because she wouldn't bring a human baby to be killed and sacrificed so they could drink the blood, but she had drunk the blood of other babies that had been sacrificed.

I had taught on the laying on of hands that night, and I was ministering at the altar when the spirit in her began to scream. I went over to her and she began to cringe and say, "No! No! Don't come near me!" I said to the spirit, "In the name of Jesus, you are going to come out of her." She screamed back at me and said, "In the name of Lucifer, I am not coming out." This scared the congregation half to death! But I just said,

Be Ye A Doer Of The Work

"You're coming out of this girl tonight. You are not going to torment her anymore. In the name of Jesus, come out of her!"

She began to scream and scream. After a few minutes, I had some of my team members gather around her and pray in the spirit — that means praying in tongues. The devil can't stand for you to pray in tongues. He can't understand what you are saying, and it drives those demons crazy. They can't stand it, so they just leave and get out of the place, and the people get set free.

After spending some time with this girl, she was completely set free from the power of Satan. After she was delivered, she came out into the lobby of the Holiday Inn, weeping and crying with the Spirit of the Lord all over her, saying, "Jesus has saved me, Jesus has saved me!" You see, when you get as deep into the works of the devil as that girl was, the devil can really get into you. He takes over your mind completely, and you will do anything he wants you to do, crazy things. But the love of God is the strongest power in the heavens and on earth. That love reached all the way into the heart of that girl and set her free. Jesus set her free and filled her with his love that night.

Now, what would have happened if I had been a hearer of the word only and had not been a doer of the work? What if I would have said, "Oh, I love you Jesus. I will teach the word for you, Jesus. But I am not going to do the work of the word and cast out devils?" That girl would have just had to go back to the Satan church and be lost forever! She would have lived forever in the pit of the damned! I could have said, "I'll be praying for you, honey. Jesus loves you." But, to be a doer of the work, I had to go over to her in the presence of the entire congregation and tell that demon, "You're not going to stay in her because I say to you in the name of Jesus to come out of her."

"No, No, No, I won't come out."

"Yes, you will. You will come out and you will come out TONIGHT."

The manager of the Holiday Inn had brought a couple of his friends to the service that night to hear me speak. They had never seen anything like that before. That night, a crippled girl walked out of her wheel chair. Just walked right out of her chair by the power of God. People were getting saved and healed all over the place. Then this girl started screaming and screaming at the top of her voice. Well, they had just never seen anything like that before. Before the night was over, the manager's friends got saved! Yeah, that's right. They got saved.

Well, that's what the Bible means when it says to be a doer of the work. You will be faced with these situations. What are you going to do? Would you just let someone else help that girl? That's what the whole church is doing. Let somebody else do it. Who? Lots of people are doers of the word. But they don't want to get involved in being a doer of the work. The first commission for the believer is to cast out devils in the name of Jesus (Mark 16). I don't know why people want to stay away from that so much. How far away from the gospel can you get! The devil is the only one who causes the human race any problems. He is the one who makes you sick, confused, broke and unhappy. You don't get any of that junk from Jesus. Use his name and fight the devil.

Be Ye A Doer Of The Work

When you get involved in being a doer of the work, you will get the promise. What does God say about the man who will be a doer of the work? He will be blessed in ALL his deeds. What a promise! How much better protection for your faith can you have than that? Blessed in all your deeds? I'll take it! If you don't want to be a doer of the work, I'll take your part and... your blessings! *"Here am I; send me" (Isa. 6:8).*

How many people do you meet these days who say to you, "Oh, I'm living by faith."

"Oh, you are? Will you go pick up Sister So&So and take her to the meeting this week?"

"Well, no, I won't be able to do that. You see, I live by faith, and my car just has so much gas in it."

"Uh, Huh. And your car is never going to have much gas in it until you get involved in being a doer of the work."

"I am believing the Lord by faith for the salvation of my husband (or wife)."

"Oh, that's wonderful. Would you go over to Sally's this week and babysit with her children for her so she can get out to the Bible Study?"

"Oh, well, no, I must feed my faith myself. I couldn't miss the meeting."

"Lady, you can protect your faith by being a doer of the work. Help Sally, and see how fast God moves in your situation. Be ye a doer of the work."

These ones who are always going around telling everyone they are living by faith, but can never help with witnessing, never pass out tracts, never cast out devils — you know what I would do if I were God? I would let them starve. He may, too! He may leave them broke long enough to get them to see the work that needs to be done and get them involved in it, and then all their deeds will begin to be blessed.

The first part of verse 25 in James, chapter one, says to continue in the perfect law of liberty. You have to be in the liberty of God to be free to do the work of God. It's wonderful to be blessed of God, but you will have to come to the place where you bypass your unbelieving relatives, you will have to bypass your unbelieving church members sitting in the pew next to you, you will pretty much have to bypass the human race as far as their believing is concerned. Don't waste your time trying to do the work of God if you are worried about offending someone with the gospel. I can tell you right now, you are going to offend some people, usually those in the church, if you stick to the gospel of Jesus Christ. But I have learned one thing about the sinner — if he sees God's power in operation, he will believe and be saved. You'll get more people to receive the Lord Jesus Christ by demonstrating the power of God than any other way. Just be bold and go ahead and demonstrate his power in the name of Jesus. And don't let those "fuddy-duddies" in the church stop you.

I was in a beautiful home here awhile back. I guess it cost about $5 million dollars. They had a swimming pool and just about everything else you could imagine. The lady of the home told me that if I wanted to go swimming, she would heat the pool for me. But as we sat there talking, this lady had the cares of the world heavy on her. She told me that she would get confused, and heavy depressions would come on her, and that, generally, her life was miserable and unhappy. The Lord spoke to me and said, "Make her stop talking like that." I just got up out of my seat and walked over to her, real calm-like, and said to her, "Now, Madam, just sit real quiet and don't be afraid. Close your eyes." What do I care if she is worth $5 million dollars? She is all messed up in her mind, and that's what I am here for, to do the work of God. I put my hands on her and said, "No, you don't, Satan. You are not going to oppress this woman. You are not going to make this woman suffer. I am not going to let you. In the name of Jesus, I command you to let this woman alone, and let her go FREE."

The joy of the Lord began to come to her, and she began praising God. Now, if I had just sat there thinking, "Oh this is such a beautiful house, and this is such a fine lady. I sure wouldn't want to offend her." If somebody needs help, help them. What difference does it make if they are surrounded by gold and crystal, swimming pools, mink and diamonds. She needed the Lord Jesus Christ, and without him, she really had nothing, anyway. But, God couldn't help her if I hadn't been willing to do the work. Why should I just sit there with the Spirit of the Lord in me wanting to help her and not be willing to do the work?

I used to not be willing. God has given me the strength and courage to be bold for him. He got rid of all that stuff in me that was keeping me in bondage and not able to operate in the perfect law of liberty. It took about 5 to 6 years to burn all that chaff out of me. Wouldn't I have been a great Christian to just sit there and let that woman suffer? I could have just patted her on the back and said, "I'll be remembering you in my prayers."

There's no use praying later. You have already shown God that you are ashamed of the gospel, and you will not be a doer of the work. How can you then be blessed in your deeds? I've been in that situation. I've walked off and gone out and gotten in my car and driven down the road, really feeling bad. I've had to say, "Oh, Lord, forgive me." Well, you need forgiveness, too.

James says in the last verse of the first chapter that pure religion that's undefiled is to visit the fatherless and widows in their afflictions. I know you can't go around town visiting all the people who are fatherless and all the widows who are afflicted. Visit the one you know who is in affliction;
   that one you know is in a dark hour,
   in a time of great trial,
   in a sorrow or with a heartache.
   Take them a word of hope.

You fellows who are married, encourage your wife to go visit the other women. Urge her to get a lady friend to go with her, and let them lay hands on the afflicted one and pray for her.
   Relieve a young mother for an afternoon.
   Bake a cake, and take it to a friend.

Call someone on the telephone and tell them that Jesus loves them. It seems to me that today, folks don't seem to care anymore. When I was small, folks used to help each other out more. God will bless you much when you reach out to bless others.

Don't ever make fun of a teenager out working the streets for Jesus. You know, they come up to you and give you a tract and ask you if you know Jesus. The best thing you can do is to give them a hug and tell

Be Ye A Doer Of The Work

and tell them that Jesus appreciates them and will bless them for their zeal. Do you know that it is mostly the so-called Christians who are the most offended when approached by these kids working the streets? Especially downtown. It's like they are ashamed to be associated with them. See, this kid just got saved, and he wants the whole world to know about Jesus. He is showing you his faith by what he is doing. If you see someone trying to do something for God, even though he might not be very smooth at it because he may be young and inexperienced and can't talk too well, he's doing what he can. But what are you doing about God's work? What he is doing is better than nothing.

James says, *"I will shew thee my faith by my works. Thou believest that there is one God; thou doest well: the devils also believe, and tremble" (Jas. 2:18,19).*

"Oh, I believe in the Lord, Brother Norvel," you say. "I love the Lord. I believe in God." Do you realize how important the work of God is? Are you involved in any "work" for him?

I understood that part in James about being a doer of the word. You know, you just can't confess with your mouth that you are healed and go around still acting sick. I knew that part. But God is saying here that you aren't really being a real doer of the word until you are involved in the "work." And your faith won't work. There is no way you can be a doer of the word without working for God. But a doer of the word and a doer of the work will be blessed in all his deeds.

Everything in your life will fall in place. The joy of the Lord will flow through you continually. The peace of God will abide with you. You won't be in and out, up and down all the time. You don't have to lose the peace of God and then try to get it back again. I used to be like that — up and down — up and down. You get so far out into left field and wonder how you got out there. I saw that I was saying that I was a believer in the word, and I thought I was a doer of the work, but I didn't have the works to back up my profession. And my faith didn't work. I prayed and asked the Lord to allow me to walk in the perfect law of liberty. I said, "Jesus, I want to be a real doer of the work. I want to cast out devils. I want to lay hands on the sick and see them recover. I want to visit the widows and the fatherless in their afflictions. I want to preach the gospel to all the world and see folks saved. I want to be a worker for you, Jesus. Set me free to work for you."

AND HE DID!

And now I am blessed in all my needs. The fields are white for harvest. I pray the Lord Jesus Christ will send forth laborers into the fields.

CHAPTER SIX

PROTECT YOUR FAITH WITH LOVE

I am going to talk real straight to you. Just open up your spirit and listen, because if you don't do what we are going to study in this chapter, you are going to stay in trouble with God your whole life. You will live a life of struggle.

The second chapter of the book of James talks about the kind of love you must have to protect your faith:
>My brethren, have not the faith of our
>Lord Jesus Christ, the Lord of glory,
>with respect of persons.

Now most all persons are guilty of this. We say we have faith, but we have respect of persons. You will have to pray for God to deliver you from this. I formerly was not able to obey the Lord in this matter. I was a Christian, but I would find myself having favor in human beings. As far as I can tell today, I do not show favor with God's people anymore. I pray to God that I do not.

God loves everybody the same. He doesn't have any pets. There is not one person on the face of the earth today that God doesn't love, that Jesus didn't die for, and whom God is willing that he or she should perish. If we are going to be like Jesus, we must love the same way. Let's continue reading in the second chapter of James:

If there come unto your assembly a man with a gold ring, in goodly apparel, and there come in also a poor man in vile raiment; And ye have respect to him that weareth the gay clothing, and say unto him, Sit thou here in a good place; and say to the poor, Stand thou there, or sit here under my footstool: Are ye not then partial in yourselves, and are become judges of evil thoughts?

Do you know that every time you show respect of persons, you do not have faith? That kind of junk will rob your faith. And the blessings of God will be far from you.

I feel sorry for churches and pastors who won't let kids with long hair go to their church. There are not 5 or 6 of these kids. There are hundreds of them. Long hair, short hair, beards, mustaches. Some ladies wear make-up, some don't. The Bible says, man looks on the outward appearance, but God looks on the heart. If God has accepted them into his family, and washed them clean of their sins, we are to accept them, too. God can finish the work he has started in a person. We are to love them without respect of persons. Romans 8:1 says, *"There is therefore now no condemnation to them which are in Christ Jesus,"* and the 13th chapter of I Corinthians says that love *"Beareth all things, believeth all things, hopeth all things, and endureth all things."*

I've seen these kids with the long hair and beards who have been on dope, free sex, and everything else, begin to weep and cry out to God. He hits them with his mighty power and they get saved and healed and everything else they need. I've seen ladies loaded down with make-up melt under the power of God, and the mascara will run all over their face. I just say, "That's okay, lady. Just enjoy the presence of the Lord." Her face will be half black with mascara. Well, God can wash that stuff off. That's not our job. Our job is to love her, without respect of persons.

You know, sometimes God will get ahold of someone and they will begin to shout. Sure does feel good. I've done it myself. Now I know that if you did that in most churches, especially on Sunday morning, they would try to quiet you down. But in the Southern Baptist church where I was raised, there was an old woman who attended the services who lived way up in the mountains. You couldn't quiet her down. No sir. She would just take a spell. That's right. Just take a spell and begin walking up and down the aisles, back and forth across the church, praising and glorifying God. She wore a long dress, and had her hair rolled up on the back of her head with great big crooked hair pins sticking through it. She wore black hi-top shiny patent-leather shoes. She would walk down that long dusty path out of the mountains to the service and along about the second verse of the first hymn, Amazing Grace, how sweet the sound, she would take a spell.

You mean, on Sunday morning?

On Sunday morning.

She would be in another world. You can't talk to someone in a spell, you know. The tears would be streaming down her face, and she would have the glory of God all over her, and you knew she was talking to Jesus. And everybody in that church knew that she was real and that she knew Jesus. Why, no one would have dared to tell her to sit down and be quiet: "Now, sister, you're interfering with the meeting."

Well, most meetings need to be interferred with!

Jesus never gets a chance to get on the program.

You have to get the people out by noon or they complain.

The roast will burn.

Why, this lady had been taking spells for years. I guess about 40 years. You could hear her up in the mountains, praising God, running through the peas, shouting and singing songs to Jesus. If the glory falls on you, you'll run through the peas praising God. And it sure feels good.

Sometime awhile back, I was at a banquet-type meeting. I had my scriptures all ready, and when I got up to speak, the Lord said, "Tell them the story about the girl who couldn't come back." I obeyed the Lord, told the story, gave the invitation, and a precious girl named Nancy came forward. The Spirit of the Lord came on her, and she took a spell. Lasted over 45 minutes. Too late for me to speak. Now, what if I had been a conventional-type fellow, a respector of persons and considered what the congregation of people would expect, and continued with the program? Nancy would have been hindered from coming to God, taking a spell and getting set free. Jesus knew she was there — a pastor's daughter who had been having dope parties in her apartment for over six years. But the Lord through the story reached out and got Nancy and brought her to the foot of the cross. He rung her out like a rag.

Protect Your Faith With Love

Most services need to be interferred with. Jesus has never lost his compassion for people in deep sin. God doesn't have any pets. Jesus loves Nancy the same as he loves Billy Graham. And he knew just exactly the words to have me say to get to Nancy. We must always stay open to the moving of the Spirit of the Lord. A message you have prepared can always be given later. I couldn't show partiality to that whole congregation and ignore the Spirit of the Lord reaching out to Nancy. No one in that service was robbed of what God had for them that night. Why, there is more rejoicing in heaven over one sinner coming home than any other event that happens on earth. Jesus said he came not to call the righteous, but sinners to repentance. The ninety and nine at that meeting witnessed the Great Shepherd leaving the flock to get the one little lamb that was lost.

The second chapter of James continues, *"But ye have despised the poor."* Ye have despised the poor. Not long ago, the Lord directed me to take some groceries to some poor folks. It was pouring down rain that night, and I carried in the two big bags of groceries. I got inside the door, and the little children were reaching up to me trying to get the food out of the bags. I looked around, and there were no bedspreads on the beds. The rain was coming through the ceiling. The little kids were dirty and had no shoes on. I asked the mother where the father was.

"Oh, I don't know. He left with some other woman. He left us." I looked at those little children, so innocent, and the Spirit of the Lord came on me to weep and pray. Oh, you know the work of the ministry covers a lot of territory. Some people wouldn't go into a place like that. I just let Jesus love those people through me. They knew that someone cared for them. You know, you can stand around and just wonder if God wants you to help people like that. I can tell you right now, he does. Don't ever wonder about it again.

I know a pastor who has the most beautiful ministry of preaching the gospel and helping the poor I have ever seen. Helping the poor is preaching the gospel. Everything you do for anybody is preaching the gospel. Jesus said, *(Matt. 25:35,36) "For I was an hungred, and ye gave me meat: I was thirsty, and ye gave me drink: I was a stranger, and ye took me in: Naked, and ye clothed me: I was sick, and ye visited me: I was in prison, and ye came unto me."*

The disciples asked, "When did we do all these things, Master?" And Jesus answered in verse 40: *"Inasmuch as ye have done it unto one of the least of these my brethren, ye have done it unto me."* This pastor told me, "I have to do it, Norvel. When God called me as a drummer out of a dance band, he told me plainly, 'I have called you to preach the gospel and to help the poor.' " When he first started his church, he gave to his members. They didn't give to him. They were starving and he fed them. He paid the rent on the building himself. He loved them.

The Bible says in James 2:6,7:

> Ye have despised the poor. Do not rich men oppress you, and draw you before the judgment seats? Do not they blaspheme that worthy name by the which ye are called?

Yes, they do. Not all of them, but most of them. You start talking about Jesus to them, and about the things

Protect Your Faith With Love

of God, and they don't want to be involved in that kind of stuff. They've got lots of money and can do whatever they want in life. And yet, if one of them shows up at church, we show them favor and want to know them, and ignore the poor little woman over in the corner with the ragged children at her knees.

The Bible says that if you fulfill the royal law according to the scriptures, you love your neighbor as yourself, you do well. Now, it's hard to love your neighbor as yourself, but you can do it. Make up your mind that you want to have the compassion of Jesus flow in and through you to people who need help. Help them, and don't look for anything in return. The Bible says that if you have respect to persons — now read this part carefully, James 2:9 — *"But if ye have respect to persons, YE COMMIT SIN!"* You have to repent of sin, you know. Look at it again. If you have respect to persons, you commit sin and are convinced of the law as transgressors. The Bible says that your neighbor is that one who comes across your path that you know needs help. You are to help them just as you would like someone to help you if you were in the same situation.

And without respect of persons.

Your "neighbor" is not just those who go to your church. Most people will only love those who are a part of "their group." But this is showing respect of persons. And it is sin. If you have a grudge against someone, you are showing respect of persons. Forgive them and forget it. Do they owe you money, and won't pay it back? Have you asked for it several times, and they just won't pay it? Forgive them the debt and forget it. Love them in Jesus and allow vengeance to be the Lord's. The word says, "I will repay."

God loves all his creation the same. Each and every person is important to him. Each and every person has a place in the body of Christ and a function to perform that is important. In fact, God says he will even give more honor to the "less comely parts" in order that none would have occasion to pride. We must not hold some in our esteem above others. We must love without discrimination. When we love without respect of persons, we remain strong in faith, and heirs of the Kingdom of God. Protect your faith with love.

CHAPTER SEVEN

PROTECT YOUR FAITH WITH WORSHIP

Mark 12:29, 30 says:
> And Jesus answered him, The first of all the commandments is, Hear, O Israel; The Lord our God is one Lord: And thou shalt love the Lord thy God with all thy heart, and with all thy soul, and with all thy mind, and with all thy strength: THIS IS THE FIRST COMMANDMENT.

One morning, as I was studying my Bible, the Lord came to me with a new message on *How To Get Your Prayers Answered.* I guess everyone in the whole world who prays would love to have Jesus come to them and tell them how to get every prayer they prayed answered. Wouldn't you love to get every single prayer you prayed answered?

Well, Jesus showed me how, and it is so simple. He said to me, "Son, the vast majority of the church members have jumped right over my first commandment. They just don't do it." I thought, "Well how is the best way to show God that you love him with all your heart, soul, mind and strength?" We show him that we love him by worshipping him. God made man, and he knew that man would worship whatever he loved. That is one reason God told the people they couldn't make an idol of any kind to represent him, because he knew they would bow down and worship the idol instead of him. He says in Exodus 34:14, *"For thou shalt worship no other god: for the Lord, whose name is Jealous, is a jealous God."*

God doesn't want you giving your love and attention to anyone or anything else except him. Not your family, not your friends, not your work, not even your ministry, if you have one. Jesus said in Luke 14:26:

If any man come to me, and hate not his father, and mother, and wife, and children, and brethren, and sisters, yea, and his own life also, he cannot be my disciple.

And Jesus finished this teaching by saying in verse 33:

So likewise, whosoever he be of you that forsaketh not all that he hath, he cannot be my disciple.

Now this doesn't mean that you are to hate your wife or your children or leave them to be a disciple of the Lord Jesus Christ. But it does mean that you can't let your love for your family or your job or even your ministry come between you and Jesus. Your love for Jesus must come first. And you must make time to worship and adore him just because he is Jesus Christ the Lord — not for what he has done for you, not for giving you a wonderful family, not for prospering you in your business, not for healing your body or saving

Protect Your Faith With Worship

your loved ones, and not for the wonderful works he is performing in the ministry he has given you.

Worship him just because he is Lord.

He died on the cross just for you.

He is worthy.

Revelation 4:11 says:

> Thou art worthy, O Lord, to receive glory and honour and power: for thou hast created all things, and for thy pleasure they are and were created.

You see, God originally created you just for his pleasure — to share all the rest of his creation with you. He made you in his image in order to have an intelligent being able to receive and understand his thoughts and ways. He did this through Jesus.

When man sinned in the Garden of Eden and died spiritually, he could no longer fellowship with God in Spirit and in truth. But now, through the blood of Jesus, we have had this spiritual fellowship restored. When we receive the Spirit of God that raised Jesus from the dead, we are quickened in our mortal flesh and made alive again: we can now give God the praise and worship he deserves and which he desires to have from all his creation.

Psalm 148 says:

> Praise ye the Lord. Praise ye the Lord from the heavens: praise him in the heights. Praise ye him, all his angels: praise ye him, all his hosts. Praise ye him, sun and moon: praise him, all ye stars of light. Praise him, ye heavens of heavens, and ye waters that be above the heavens. Let them praise the name of

the Lord: for he commanded, and they were created. Praise the Lord from the earth, ye dragons and all deeps: fire and hail; snow and vapour; stormy wind fulfilling his word: mountains, and all hills; fruitful trees, and all cedars: beasts, and all cattle; creeping things, and flying fowl; Kings of the earth, and all people; princes, and all judges of the earth: both young men, and maidens; old men, and children: Let them praise the name of the Lord: for his name alone is excellent; his glory is above the earth and heaven.

Psalm 149 continues:

Praise ye the Lord. Sing unto the Lord a new song, and his praise in the congregation of saints.

I would say that the vast majority of the gospel services of the churches on the earth do not please God because of the organized services they hold. It does not please God to hold services in such a manner. The one thing that pleases God more than anything else is for him to see his people worshipping him. I don't think that any church or church member can know the abundant life with the full blessings of God resting on them, walking in health and financial blessings, and all the things that God has promised in his word, if they are not going to spend time worshipping him. He said for his praise to be in the congregation of saints.

Probably full-gospel churches praise God better than most folks, but even then, too often the pastor will say, "Just raise your hands and praise the Lord," and they praise the Lord for about 30 to 60 seconds, and then it is on with the program.

Now, if the saints don't spend time worshipping the Lord, their prayers are cut off and faith is cut off. In fact, our faith can become so damaged before God that we can't receive anything. Especially full-gospel Christians. I see folks all the time come up to the altar at my services begging God for a healing. They have been begging him for this healing for years. They can't understand why they don't get it. But they haven't protected their faith by spending time worshipping God.

When you go into most church services today, they are all sitting around talking to each other in the natural language, in their natural minds. Well, the natural man understandeth not the things of God. And they are talking in the natural mind about some conversation they had last week, or about their garden, or their new clothes, "Oh, Sally, that is such a pretty dress you have on." "Thank you, I bought it at a So&So exclusive Dress Shoppe."

So you have a pretty dress on, big deal. Maybe you have ten tailor-made suits in your closet. So what? You might look good on the street, but that doesn't help you any with God. But when you come to church, if the people come into the sanctuary in the Spirit of the Lord with the spirit of worship on them, and bow down at their seats or at the altar and begin to worship God and seek his face with all their heart, everything is so easy. Actually, the congregation should begin to prepare their hearts to worship Jesus before they get to the church building. You see, you are the temple of the Living God, and YOU bring God to church. God isn't automatically there because the sign on the outside says "church building." Either you bring him into the building made with bricks and stones or he doesn't inhabit.

The scriptures say that God inhabits the praises of his people in Psalm 22:3. 1 Peter 2:5 says, *"Ye also, as lively stones, are built up a spiritual house, an holy priesthood, to offer up spiritual sacrifices, acceptable to God by Jesus Christ."* Hebrews 13:15 says, *"By him therefore let us offer the sacrifice of praise to God continually, that is, the fruit of our lips giving thanks to his name."* Hebrews 2:12 quotes Jesus as saying, *"I will declare thy name unto my brethren, in the midst of the church will I sing praise unto thee."*

Oh, if the CHURCH would only give these praises to God, I doubt if the pastor would even have to preach too much. People would just get saved and healed in their seats. God would come down and inhabit the praises of the people and meet all their needs. Now, remember, when we don't worship like we should, things go hard for us. Life will be a continual struggle, and God doesn't want you to struggle. Just give him everything,

. . . your cares and worries
. . . your needs in your body and soul
. . . your unsaved loved ones
. . . your money problems
. . . cast all of your cares on him for he careth for you
. . . and then spend time worshipping him.

Praising him.

Thanking him.

Give him his place as Lord of Lords and King of Kings.

He is a faithful creator. He doesn't just have love. He is love. His whole nature is to love, to cherish, to

Protect Your Faith With Worship

protect, to provide all of the needs of his children. And the church walks around today sick, poor, depressed and oppressed. Where is the light? Where is the salt?

Actually, if each one of us would spend time worshipping Jesus at home alone, we would be better able to worship him together with the other saints when we come together at church. I'll tell you that when I spend time worshipping the Lord by myself, just praising him for who he is and not for what he has done for me, not taking any time to ask him for anything, just thanking him for saving me and dying on the cross in my place – why, my life is so easy. Everything just falls in place. I can't explain it. But there is no struggle, no wondering why God doesn't do something for me. He takes care of everything. He gives me financial deals. He provides me people to help me with the businesses so I can preach and teach for him as much as he wants. I just can't emphasize this point enough.

Worship will protect your faith more than anything else you can do. Yes, joy will protect your faith. Giving properly will protect your faith. Your confession must be in line with God's word and you must be a doer of the work. You must have God's love flowing through you by the Holy Spirit, but if your life is a life of worship, you can please God in a way that you have probably never known before. He's looking at you every day, you know, and if you're pleasing him with your life, everything will be so easy. You can't please God more than by spending time worshipping him every day. Your faith will be completely protected from all forces of darkness and the devil in all ways. Worship is the greatest protector of your faith there is. Make your life a life of worship.

If you wish to begin this life of worship today, here are some instructions from my own personal experience that should help you begin.

God says in John 4:24 that *"God is a spirit, and they that worship him must worship him in spirit and in truth."* In order to worship him in the spirit, you must have the baptism with the Holy Spirit. Jesus said in John 15:26 that he would send the Comforter and that the Holy Spirit would glorify Jesus. So to properly glorify the Lord Jesus Christ, we should give him priase through the Holy Spirit. Romans 8:8, 9 says, *"They that are in the flesh cannot please God. But ye are not in the flesh, but in the Spirit, if so be that the Spirit of God dwell in you."* Acts 2:4 shows that the evidence of having the Spirit of God is speaking in tongues. And Ephesians 5:18, 19 and 20 says that when we are filled with the Spirit, we can sing to the Lord in psalms and hymns and spiritual songs, giving thanks always for all things unto God and the Father in the name of our Lord Jesus Christ.

Now, pick a time during the day when you are alone.

All of us have a time even if it is just those minutes in the shower each morning. Or driving to work in the car. Or when the baby is taking his nap. Each of us has a moment during the day when we can get alone with the Lord. If you can't find any time, get up an hour earlier each morning, or take time before you go to bed at night. Go before the Lord and begin to offer up the spiritual sacrifices of praise in the Spirit. Let your spirit begin to praise God through your mouth, praying in the Spirit and glorifying God. If you have never praised God in the Spirit, just begin to offer up your voice to him and don't speak in a language you know. The Holy

Spirit will give you a Spirit language in which to praise God and glorify Jesus. That is his office in the church today. He will perform his office through any yielded child of God who will believe, in faith. Your job is to speak and his job is to give you the words to speak. The scripture says in Acts 2:4, *And they were all filled with the Holy Ghost, and began to speak with other tongues, as the Spirit gave them utterance."*

Then, as you pray in the Spirit, begin to bring your mind to concentrate on Jesus. The scripture says that as you pray in the Spirit, the understanding is unfruitful (1 Cor. 14:14). Your mind will tend to wander over everything. Allow the Spirit of God to magnify Jesus and control your mind. *"Bringing into captivity every thought to the obedience of Christ,"* the scriptures say in 2 Cor. 10:5. Make your mind concentrate on the cross. Picture the price Jesus paid for you to bring you to God. Begin to see Jesus sitting at the right hand of God the Father, making intercession for you. Soon, as you continue praising God through your spirit, your whole soul and body will begin to be one with the Spirit. Your whole being will begin to be involved in praising the Lord. You will be taken out of this earthly, natural plane and will be able to enter into the heavenlies in the Spirit.

Once you experience this entrance into the holy presence of the Lord Jesus Christ, you will never be the same again. I promise you that. The holy presence of God will melt you down. Your whole life will be different. Your whole attitude towards others will begin to be different. Your life will begin to be a glorious and wonderful moment by moment experience with your beloved. Your faith will be protected by the heights and depths, the length and breadth of the love of God.

EPILOGUE

MY PRAYER

Lord Jesus, I wish to have my life be a life of faith, for your word says that the just shall live by faith, and when you come again, you will be looking for that one element in the life of the born-again person that is pleasing to you, FAITH.

Help me to protect my faith with joy. Help me to protect my life by giving of myself and my substance to you to preach the gospel. I lay down my life at your feet, Jesus. Take me and use me. Make me a doer of the work. Help me to love all of your church with the same love you love them with, forgiving them, rejoicing not in their falls, praying for them, all the same, Jesus, like you do.

And most of all, Lord Jesus, help me to worship you as I should. Father, in the precious name of Jesus, I am your love-slave to do whatever you want me to do. Make me a fit vessel for your holy presence and manifest me forth to a lost and dying world as a son in the full measure of the stature of the first-begotten Son, the Lord Jesus Christ, in whose life I am hidden and with whose faith I live. Amen.

_____

Your Name

_____

Date

Norvel Hayes shares God's Word boldly and simply, with an enthusiasm that captures the heart of the hearer. He has learned through personal experience that God's Word can be effective in every area of life and that it will work for anyone who will believe it and apply it.

Norvel owns several businesses which function successfully despite the fact that he spends over half his time away from the office, ministering the Gospel throughout the country.

His obedience to God and his willingness to share his faith has taken him to a variety of places. He ministers in churches, seminars, conventions, colleges, prisons—anywhere the Spirit of God leads.

For a complete list of tapes and books
by Norvel Hayes, write:

Norvel Hayes
P. O. Box 1379
Cleveland, TN 37311

*Feel free to include your prayer requests
and comments when you write.*

Books by Norvel Hayes

How to Live and Not Die

You Can Be A Soulwinner

Jesus Taught Me to Cast Out Devils

Prosperity Now!

God's Boot Camp

God's Power Through the Laying On of Hands

How To Protect Your Faith

7 Ways Jesus Heals

The Blessing of Obedience

Stand In The Gap For Your Children

How To Get Your Prayers Answered

What To Do For Healing

Holy Spirit Gifts Series

Number One Way To Fight The Devil

Why You Should Speak In Tongues

Available at your local bookstore.

Harrison House
P. O. Box 35035 • Tulsa, OK 74153